TH.
DISAPPEARANCE

THERESA MARRAMA

DEDICATION

This book is dedicated to everyone out there who helps to pass on stories from generation to generation. You are the ones that help keep legends alive. Legends should never be discarded or treated as unimportant. Keep sharing your stories and keep allowing others the chance to believe.!

TABLE OF CONTENTS

ACKNOWLEDGMENTS

I would like to thank Gayla LePage for taking the time to read and edit my story!

PROLOGUE

Her best friend is not here. Where is she? It is a question that everyone in New York has asked in the last week.

Now Anne is alone, but the disappearance of her best friend haunts her every night. It is a horrible dream; a nightmare that repeats day after day.

CHAPTER ONE

IN FRONT OF HER LOCKER

It is 5:30 at night. I am alone in the school. I look at the locker in front of me. There are a lot of pictures and cards. There are a lot of flowers and plants on the floor in front of the locker.

I am in front of my friend's locker. Not just my friend, but my best friend. I am alone. There isn't anyone at school. I am alone with my thoughts.

Without you, Dominique, everything is different. Without you, I am all alone.

At school, my locker is next to her locker. On my locker, there is nothing. I look at Dominique's locker. I look at all the flowers and plants on the floor in front of the locker. Everyone at school thinks about Dominique a lot. People put flowers and plants in front of her locker. People put letters and photos because they want to respect Dominique. The situation is sad. Everything is sad. It is sad like me.

I walk toward some of the flowers in front of her locker. I look at them and at that moment I see something strange. I see one flower alone on the ground. This flower was not there this morning. This flower is not like the other flowers in front of her locker. It is red but there is something attached to the flower. I see a photo. There is a photo of Dominique attached to the flower. It is a selfie. It is a selfie of her in the forest a week ago.

The photo paralyzes me. I don't like the fact that she is not here. I don't like that she has disappeared. I don't like not understanding what happened to my best friend. I don't like to see flowers and letters for Dominique everywhere. I don't like this situation. I don't like my life without my best friend. I don't like it! I don't like it at all!

So, I run. I run toward the door in order to leave the school. I run quickly, without breathing. I run without thinking. I run. I get to the door. I panic! Finally, I breathe. I breathe; and I look at her locker again. I see the flower. I see the photo of her in the forest.

Why is the photo there? Why a photo of Dominique in the forest? Who put the photo there? Even more important, why this photo?

I look at her locker in silence and think about Dominique and the phrase that she repeats in my dream, the same dream. Since Dominique disappeared I have the same dream and hear the same phrase, night after night.

- Alice we have to talk; it is important!

What does she want to talk about? No, it is only a dream. A dream that haunts me.

At that moment, I run toward her locker. I take the flower with the photo of Dominique. While I walk toward my house it is windy. There is wind and a horrible noise. I have the flower and the photo in my hand. The flower flies in the wind but I still have the photo in my hand. I walk quickly towards my house while looking at the photo. I only hear the wind, the wind that is howling like wolves.

CHAPTER 2
WORRIES

It is six thirty at night. My father is home. It is not normal. He is never home but today he is here. I live with my dad. I don't have any brothers or sisters. My mother died when I was a baby. When my father is home, I panic. I panic because he always asks a lot of questions. Today, I want to be alone. I see my father in the living room. I don't go in the living room. My father is on the phone. I listen to the conversation. I wonder who he is on the phone with?

- *Yes, everything is very difficult. I work all day. I work every day. I don't have time for anything.*

I think to myself. *It is true ! You don't have time for anything, and you definitely don't have time for me.*

- *Alice ? It is even more difficult. She is not at home often. She is at school every day. And when she is home, she is in her bedroom. She doesn't say anything. She never talks to me.*

Who doesn't talk? Me? Who do you want me to talk to? You?

- No, I didn't call a therapist.

A therapist? Really? I don't need a therapist. I need my best friend!

- There is a therapist at school; maybe I can call her. I know that I can't talk to her. I don't know what to do. I am her father, but she doesn't want to talk to me about her problems. She doesn't listen to me. She never listens to me.

Really? I can't talk to you because you are never home. You are always working!

- Yes, she is young. Alice is only 15 years old. She doesn't have any sisters or brothers to talk to. Poor

Alice, she doesn't have a mom. Now her best friend is not here. I don't know what to do.

You don't know what to do! I don't know what to do!

- She can't be alone. Yes, I understand. I don't' know what to do, but I need to work. There is a girl who disappeared!

Yes, I can be alone! I am almost an adult! I am 15 years old. I am alone most of the time when you are working!

- Yes, it is an important decision, but finding Dominique is the most important thing right now.

Finding my best friend is important. It is the most important thing right now!

CHAPTER 3

FEAR

It is eight o'clock at night, and my dad is not home. It is normal. Everything is different without Dominique, but my father is not home. That is not different. I am alone. My father is always working. I am always alone since Dominique disappeared. I walk in the kitchen and there is a note on the table. It is a note from my father.

Alice,

I am working late today. You have to walk the dog.
There is a pizza in the fridge for dinner.
Call me, if there is a problem!

See you later,
Dad

What? I have to walk the dog? In the dark? I am alone; I don't want to walk the dog alone. I am scared! I am scared of the dark, but if I don't walk the dog he is going to pee in the house. Do I go or not go?

My house is surrounded by a forest. It is surrounded by trees. There are a lot of trees, but small and big. I live in New York State, in the Adirondacks.

I don't want to go outside alone in the dark. I am not going to go out there. I am not brave. I am scared. I am scared of the dark. I don't like the dark! It is normal to be afraid of the dark, especially here in the Adirondacks and if one knows the legend of the Boogeyman! If you grow up in New York, you know the legend of the Boogeyman. Everyone who lives in the United States knows the legend of the Boogeyman!

CHAPTER 4

IN THE FOREST

It is eight thirty at night. I am going outside because the dog almost peed in the house. I am walking alone in the dark with

Max, my father's dog. I have Max's leash in my hand. I think about Dominique before she disappeared. We spent a lot of time together. I didn't walk the dog alone. Dominique was with me. Tonight she is not there. I walk toward the trees in the forest. I walk slowly, and I think about Dominique. She wasn't scared of anything. She wasn't scared of the dark like me!

Dominique, why am I not more like you? You are brave and strong! I am neither strong nor brave.

I continue to walk slowly in the forest. Everything is dark and silent, but I am not calm. I am scared. I walk without looking around me. I walk without looking at the trees. I only look at Max. I don't want to know if there is someone or something in the forest with me. I am scared! I think about the Boogeyman. All of a sudden, I hear a loud noise in the distance. I hear another noise and another.

I look at Max he stops immediately. I know that he hears the noise also. I think that he is scared. I know that I am scared. Max looks in the direction of the noise and I am paralyzed with fear. At that moment, I think about the day when Dominique disappeared.

Why did she go out alone that day? There was a reason. I am going to find out the truth.

I look at Max, and I turn around. I turn in the direction of my house. I run. I run faster than ever toward my house. I run without looking around me. I don't think. I can't breathe. I run quickly, and Max runs quickly in front of me.

I open the door and I enter the house. Max enters too. I close the door as fast as possible and finally I can breathe. Ahhh!

Only now I am thinking about the legend again. I am thinking about the Boogeyman and about Dominique who disappeared without a trace a week ago.

CHAPTER 5

THE LEGEND OF THE BOOGEYMAN

The legend of the Boogeyman is well known in the United States. Everyone knows this legend. Some people think that the Boogeyman exists and others don't think he exists.

Me? I don't know if the Boogeyman exists. Does the Boogeyman live in the forest, the forest behind my house?

When I was a little girl, my father told me the legend of the Boogeyman. According to the legend, the Boogeyman is a scary creature that only comes out at night. According to the legend, the Boogeyman hides under the bed of children who do not behave or in the forest or woods behind their house. The Boogeyman is very dangerous, and can kill people and animals. Many believe that it is just a way for adults to scare children into good behavior.

The night that Dominique disappeared, there was a full moon. It was a Friday the 13th. Dominique went into the forest, but she didn't come back.

Time is going by, but not quickly. Time goes by slowly. Since Dominique's disappearance, everything is going by slowly, the days, the hours, the minutes and the seconds.

CHAPITRE 6

THE UNFOREGETTABLE DREAM

It is six o'clock at night. There is no one in the house, except me. My father is working. I don't hear anything. There is a lot of silence in the house. All of a sudden,

I hear *ring-ring*, It is my cellphone. It scares me. I look at it and see – **The Police Station.** I answer.

- Hi dad.

- Hi Alice. Are you ok?

- Yes, I am ok.

- Did you eat some pizza for dinner?

- Yes, I ate a little bit of pizza.

In reality, I didn't eat. I wasn't hungry. Since Dominque disappeared, I haven't eaten a lot.

- Did you walk the dog for me?

- Yes.

If you weren't working so much, you could walk your dog in the dark.

- O.K. so don't forget to lock the door tonight. Do you hear me ?

I don't answer him immediately.

- Alice? Are you there? Do you hear me?

- Yes. I hear you. Bye.

My father is a police officer. He calls me all the time when he is working late. Last week, he started to call me more and more. After Dominique disappeared, he started to work more. Now, he works more on the investigation of her disappearance. I don't know if he works more and more because she was my best friend or because she is the first young girl who has disappeared in our town. But if anyone can find Dominique, it is my father. He is a good investigator. He is the best investigator in New York.

Everyone continues to look for Dominique. There are a lot of people who are looking for her. They look for her in the morning., in the afternoon, and at night. They don't stop looking for her.

It is eleven o'clock at night, and I am tired. I go in my bedroom. I walk toward my bed when I see the photo of Dominique that I found at school today.

Who put this photo in front of her locker?

I try to sleep, but I can't. I can't because there is a lot of noise outside. There is a terrible wind. I only hear the wind howling like wolves. I let my imagination run wild.

What time is it?

I look at the time. It is midnight. There

is a complete silence in the house, but I can hear "*tic-toc*", *tic-toc*". I am scared. The silence amplifies all the normal noises of the night in my imagination. I think about the last day I saw Dominique.

CHAPTER 7

THE DISAPPEARANCE

It was one week ago. It is Friday the 13th. Dominique and I are at school. As usual, we are together in class. We have the same classes at school. During lunch, Dominique said to me:

- Alice we have to talk; it is important!

- O.K. What do you want to talk about?

- The other night I saw the Boogeyman. It is not a legend! The Boogeyman exists!

- What? The Boogeyman? It is just a legend, Dominique. The Boogeyman doesn't exist.

- Alice, I understand, and I know that everyone says that it is only a legend. There was someone or something walking in the forest

near my house, and it resembled the Boogeyman.

- I think that it was just an animal, not the Boogeyman. I don't think that the Boogeyman exists, Dominique. Our parents tell us the legend of the Boogeyman to scare us. Our parents didn't want us walking alone in the forest at night. It's dangerous!

Dominique doesn't answer me immediately. She thinks in silence. She has a strange expression. She seems worried. She didn't mention the Boogeyman anymore.

After school, Dominique and I are walking home. We walk home from school all the time. We have to walk in the forest in order to get home. That day, Dominique didn't talk as much as usual. She walks in silence, but she walks faster than usual. I say to her, "Dominique why are you walking so fast?"

She looks at me, but continues to walk.

- I yell; Dominique stop! You need to explain to me why you seem so worried today. I don't understand.

Finally, she stops walking. She starts to explain to me.

- I can't explain it. I don't know why but I am hearing noises. I hear a lot of noises at night, Alice.

- I don't understand. What is this noise?

- I hear a howling. I think that it is the howls of an animal. At night when I hear the noises, I can't sleep.

I can see that she is nervous. She seems worried. I don't know what to say, but I know that I have to reassure her that everything is going to be alright.

- Don't worry, Dominique. I am sure that you are just hearing the noises of a dog in the forest. There are a lot of dogs around the forest. I usually hear dogs at night.

She looks at me for a moment. She doesn't respond. We continue to walk. We walk in silence until we get home.

The last thing that I said to her that day was, "Dominique, call me tonight after dinner, and we can continue to talk about it if you want!" Dominique never called me that night. The next day my father tells me that she disappeared, and that the police and the community are looking for her. He asks me a lot of questions about my last day with Dominique. He asks me a lot of questions about my last conversation with Dominique. I explain everything to him.

Dominique, where are you? Why haven't you called me?

CHAPTER 8

A PHONE CALL IN THE NIGHT

It is one o'clock in the morning when I look at the time. I can't sleep. I look out the window of my bedroom. I see the moon. The moon is shining brightly in the sky. At

that moment, I hear *ring-ring*; it's my cell phone. It scares me. I look at it and I see--
Dominique.

Dominique? Is it possible? Is it possible that Dominique is calling me?

I have my cell phone in my hand. My hand is trembling. I am paralyzed by fear.

It's only Dominique. Why am I scared? It's my best friend. I'm not scared of my best friend.

I look at my cell phone, and slowly I answer it. "Hello?" Nobody responds. I repeat, "Hello, Dominique? Hello? Are you there? Is it you?"

Nobody responds. I can't breathe. My hand is trembling. All of a sudden, I hear a howling. It is a noise unlike any other. It scares me. Silence! There is nobody on the other line. There is nobody on the other line anymore. I don't hear anything, only silence.

At that moment, there is a noise in the distance. It is a door opening. And after, the door slams! BAM! The fear paralyzes me. I can't breathe. I hear footsteps. The footsteps are in front of my bedroom door. I close my eyes. I can't breathe. My hands are trembling, and I hear a voice. It is my father's voice.

- Alice? Are you sleeping?

I slowly open my eyes, and I see my dad next to my bed.

- Dad? Is it you? Oh no, I am not sleeping. I can't sleep. Dominique called me.

- Huh? Alice why didn't you call me?

- I was scared. I couldn't breathe, dad. And, moment later you were in my bedroom.

- What did she say? What happened?

- … Nothing…

- Nothing? I don't understand.

- I was in my bed and I couldn't sleep when I heard *ring-ring*, it was my cell phone. It scared me. I looked at it and I saw –***Dominique.*** When I answered it, there wasn't anyone on the other line.

- You didn't talk to Dominique? There wasn't anyone on the other line?

- No, there wasn't anyone on the other line. I only heard the howling of an animal. It was strange.

- A howling? O.K. Alice, I need your cell phone. I have to go to the police station with this information. It is important.

You want my cell phone, but what happens if Dominique tries to call me again?

- No dad. I need my cell phone.

- I understand that you are worried, Alice, but your cell phone can help us find Dominique. It's important!

I don't say anything. I give him my cell phone. He takes it and leaves my bedroom in silence.

36

Dominique, what is happening?

Chapter 9

Her return

It's seven o'clock in the morning. I had the same dream. It's always the same dream since Dominique disappeared without a trace. She repeats the same sentence.

- Alice we have to talk; it is important!

What does she want to talk about? The words haunt me. The dream haunts me.

I can't stay home. I have to talk to my dad. I have to help find Dominique. I go to the police station. When I get there, everyone is in a panic. Everyone is talking, and I hear my dad's voice. I see

a police officer running towards the door of the police station. I see another police officer who seems worried. I see another police officer who is on the telephone.

There is a panic in the police station. When I enter, more police officers are running towards the door. In the distance, I see my dad with another person. He is talking to another investigator. My dad seems serious, and the other investigator seems worried. They are talking very fast, but I can't understand the conversation. I try to listen. I hear a little bit. I only understand, *"Yes... she is home... Yes... this morning... No... not now..."*

At that moment, I understand everything. Dominique is back! I run towards my dad. He doesn't see me immediately. Finally, when I approach him he sees me. He looks at me very confused and says to me:

40

- Alice ! What are you doing here? Is everything ok?

-    Dad.   Where   is   she? Dominique? Is she in danger? Dad! Tell me!

- Alice, calm down. I can explain. Dominique isn't in danger. She is home.

- She is home? I don't understand. When did she come home?

At that moment, I am panicked. I can't breathe. I have a lot of emotions. The situation is confusing me. I am happy that my best friend has come home. I am nervous. I look at my dad, and I start to cry. My dad puts his hand on my head and starts to walk. He walks in his office. I walk behind him.

- Alice, there are still a lot of questions. There are still a lot of things that I don't understand. Her mother called me early this morning and explained to me that Dominique was in her room sleeping. She is not in danger.

I don't say anything. I think about Dominique.

She was in her room? She was sleeping? Dominique, what happened? Where were you the last week?

CHAPTER 10

AN IMPORTANT VISIT

After a few minutes, I run. I run towards the door of the police station. I run quickly, without breathing. I run, but the only thing I can think about is Dominique. I have to talk to her. I have to understand why she disappeared without a trace. I have to know the truth.

I arrive at her house. I am panicking! Finally, I breathe. I breathe and knock on the door. The door opens, and I see her mother. A few minutes later, I am in Dominique's bedroom.

Why did you disappear? Where were you?

I look at Dominique silently. She
looks at me. She looks at me without any

expression. I want to hug her, but instead I look at her hands and her arms. I see something strange. I see scrapes and bruises, a lot of scrapes and bruises. She seems tired and sick.

Dominique, what happened? Why do you have those scrapes and bruises?

At that moment, I understand that there are a lot of things I don't know about my best friend.

She doesn't look at me. She is on her bed looking out the window in silence. Finally, she speaks.

- Alice we have to talk; it is important!

Oh no. The words that haunt me! I understand now what happened! I know exactly what she is going to say!

45

She looks at me and says what I dreaded.

- He exists. The Boogeyman isn't just a legend. The Boogeyman exists.

ABOUT THE AUTHOR

Theresa Marrama is a French teacher in Northern New York. She has been teaching French to middle and high school students for 11 years. She has translated a variety of Spanish comprehensible readers into French. She has also published books in French, Spanish and German. She enjoys teaching with Comprehensible Input and writing comprehensible stories for language learners.

CHECK OUT HER WEBSITE FOR MORE RESOURCES AND MATERIALS TO ACCOMPANY HER BOOKS:

www.compelllinglanguagecorner.com

HER BOOKS INCLUDE:

Une Obsession dangereuse, which can be purchased at www.fluencymatters.com

HER FRENCH BOOKS ON AMAZON INCLUDE:

Une disparition mystérieuse
L'île au trésor:
Première partie: La malédiction de l'île
Oak
La lettre
Léo et Anton

HER SPANISH BOOKS ON AMAZON

INCLUDE:

La ofrenda de Sofía
Una desaparición misteriosa
La Carta
Luis y Antonio

HER GERMAN BOOKS ON AMAZON

INCLUDE:

Leona und Anna
Geräusche im Wald

Made in the USA
Columbia, SC
19 June 2024